THE VISION SPLENDID

Best wishes

Dinah Livingstone

By Dinah Livingstone

Poetry Books:
Poems of Hampstead Heath and Regent's Park (2012)
Kindness (2007)
Presence (2003)
Time on Earth: Selected and New Poems (1999)
May Day (1997)
Second Sight (1993)
Keeping Heart (1989)
Saving Grace (1987)

Poetry Pamphlets:
St Pancras Wells (1991)
Something Understood (1985)
Glad Rags (1983);
Love in Time (1982)
Prepositions and Conjunctions (1977)
Ultrasound (1974)
Maranatha (1969)
Tohu Bohu (1968)
Beginning (1967)

Prose:
Poetic Tales (2010)
The Poetry of Earth (2000)
Poetry Handbook for Readers and Writers (1992)

Edited:
This Life on Earth (2009)
Work: An Anthology (1999)
Camden Voices Anthology 1978–1990 (1990)

The Vision Splendid

Dinah Livingstone

KATABASIS

First published on May 12th 2014
by KATABASIS
10 St Martin's Close, London NW1 0HR
katabasis@katabasis.co.uk
www.katabasis.co.uk
Copyright © Dinah Livingstone 2014
Designed and typeset in-house mainly in 12 point Garamond
Printed in England by imprintdigital.com
Front cover image: Reredos batik by Thetis Blacker:
The Tree of Life in the New Jerusalem, St Botolph without Aldgate

ISBN: 978-0-904872-47-7
Trade Distribution: Central Books
99 Wallis Road
London E9 5LN
(0845 458 9911)

British Library Cataloguing in Publication Data:
A catalogue record for this book is available
from the British Library.

Acknowledgments

Thank you very much indeed to the artist Thetis Blacker, together with St Botolph's without Aldgate and its helpful administrator Nigel Sharp, for permission to take and use a photo of the reredos batik of *The Tree of Life in the New Jerusalem* for the front cover image of this book.

Many thanks to Kathleen McPhilemy and Grace Livingstone for reading the proofs.

Some of these poems were first published in *Acumen, Morning Star, The Interpreter's House*.

NOTE

Some poems belonging to this collection were first published in Dinah Livingstone's *Poems of Hampstead Heath and Regent's Park* (Katabasis 2012) to complete the calendar.

Contents

Forewords

'What do you want?' Jesus asked him.
'Lord, I want to see.'

— BLIND BARTIMAEUS,
Mark 10:51

*

'London, my most kindly nurse'

— EDMUND SPENSER,
Prothalamion

*

'And by the vision splendid
Is on the way attended'

— WILLIAM WORDSWORTH,
Ode on Intimations of Immortality

*

'Yes, surely! And if others can see it as I have seen it, then it may be called a vision rather than a dream.'

— WILLIAM MORRIS,
News from Nowhere

The fields from Islington to Marybone,
To Primrose Hill and Saint John's Wood,
Were builded over with pillars of gold
And there Jerusalem's pillars stood.

Her little ones ran on the fields,
The Lamb of God among them seen,
And fair Jerusalem his Bride
Among the little meadows green.

Pancras and Kentish Town repose
Among her golden pillars high,
Among her golden arches which
Shine upon the starry sky.

The Jew's harp house and the Green Man,
The ponds where boys to bathe delight,
The fields of cows by Willan's farm,
Shine in Jerusalem's pleasant sight …

Is this thy soft family love
They cruel patriarchal pride,
Planting thy family alone,
Destroying all the world beside? …

In my exchanges every land
Shall walk, and mine in every land
Mutual shall build Jerusalem
Both heart in heart and hand in hand.

— WILLIAM BLAKE,
Jerusalem

Joint Operation

Healing happens like spring,
creeps up, hesitates,
steals another march, leaps,
settles in her lap,
then, distracted, disappears
and she thinks she's lost it.

But slowly her body remembers
how it feels to walk normally
and she wants to rejoin the world.
Is there anybody there?

She'd like to say what she sees,
how it is with her.
Who to? To you. Another.
Hear me as I hear you,
holding to what you are.
Please hold me too.

Alone is the essence of damnation.
What is the point
of talking, walking,
if it is not towards?

Crying

Half asleep I catch myself sobbing.
Is there a flood behind that gothic door?
Now it creaks and through a crack
tears trickle. Childhood woes
I was told then I had no right to feel –
you are a bad girl – ache again
in inchoate unwantedness.

Hell's fury roars;
should I yank the door open
to let out the whole of it?
But before I can, it reseals tight
and thwarted, I'm relieved.
Mightn't those waters drown me,
destroy bystanders besides?

Come the morning something shifts,
channels itself; that inarticulate
No is now the same dark energy
generating hydroelectric power
that surges into Yes.

Words form:
Let there be light
to live, belong, to love unquenchably.
The surge hums.
Could it become a poem?

Fallow

The field is lying fallow.
Tall red clover, plantain
and coarse grass have taken over.
Nothing but weeds
but they thrive in the sun regardless.
'Weed is a rude word,'
said the brickie mending my wall;
'it's plant racism.'

Perhaps he was right.
My mind felt exhausted and barren.
I went to the country
without any plans implanted.
Resting from rota and furrow
I idled out here on a sunny morning.
Later, as if out of nowhere,
up popped this poem.

What Do You Mean?

'In itself the universe is meaningless,'
I heard a sophist say.
Where would he be, I wondered,
if it took umbrage, went away?
Bereft not only of Oxford,
but with nothing left at all,
not even himself to lord it and survey.
If the sun and moon should doubt
they'd immediately go out,
when self-belief failed.

I sit in a Suffolk field that is growing
potatoes, every thrusting leafiness
proclaims from its furrow: I AM
and here on this bank, pointy-brown plantain
with its creamy halo of stamens,
a clump of red campion,
clear-eyed, sky-blue speedwell,
extravagant curling vetch
and briefly the brilliant poppy,
each unique life transits its time: I AM.

I walk through my home park.
That patch has populated itself
with wild barley from who knows where,
while a loud iridescence of starlings,
an uprising of roses, London plane
and sycamore rocked by the stiff breeze,
whooshing, wafting, raucously,
re-echo: I AM, I AM, I AM.

Their being is their own,
not ours to impose.
What we can do as speaking animals
belonging to that one economy
is listen, suffer them in their thisness,
then give them a human voice
with a place in our poetry.

What the Welsh Walnut Tree Said

Day of meetings, unmeetings,
exhaustion of nitty gritty,
what did not get said.
Late lumbered deep
into slumbering dark.

Now I wake in Wales
with morning breaking
a gauzy azure set to clear.

A sturdy walnut tree stands at my window,
whose clean-cut, day-lit, lingual leaves
wave at me speakingly:
Up, lump. Come, undumb
yourself and me.

Crocuses in St Martin's Gardens

River of being in full spate,
ungainsayable, itself, *olé!*
Purple, white and yellow crocuses
up, over and then down
in a broad band through green
throng this spring morning.

I stand in the sun and marvel.
All I can say is yes
to being here and being alive,
which blooms into belief
love is the word.

For now I am on crutches.
I'm getting old and suffer loneliness.
Under that grassy mound
in this old graveyard
are buried heaps of bones,
including Nell Gwyn's, they say.

The passionate crocus colours
will not stay but nevertheless …

Late

November roses persist on leggy stems.
Soft dawn-pink they stand
out in the cold light
that penetrates the thinning trees
to fall on soggy bright green grass
and drifts of leaves forgone.

Their ragged blooms hit home;
I cheer. Diminished and near death
they keep their counsel and their dignity.

Sorrow

It pierces or it scorches
like a heart-shaped flat iron,
the sharp pain of seeing
someone you love suffer
grief, or harsh,
bitter disappointment,
when you can do
nothing about it,
say nothing to change it,
and even feeling all that hurt
yourself, not sleeping,
makes it no better.
In the dead of winter
you can only wait.

For Sale by Auction

Hopeful couples looking for a home
compete with astute professionals,
who snap their tiny cameras like jaws.
'You could throw an ensuite here.
Of course, extend into the loft.'

Drawn by the starting price,
they arrive on the viewing day.
The small Victorian house
suffers them like an old grey mare.
It has become a slum,
damp, grimy, with a wicked crack
down the main front wall.

The anonymous owner lived here 37 years.
She's left some interesting books,
a good walnut chest of drawers,
imposing double bed.
The kitchen has a cat flap. In the garden
two empty bird feeders dangle forlorn.

I wonder about her life.
Was it rich with meaning, full of love?
Was she widowed, left alone?
Did she struggle to carry on in the place
where she felt she belonged
but could no longer afford to maintain?
Did she feel just too old?

'The property requires underpinning,'
says the agent. 'You're looking at 100k.'
The dealers will have factored that in,
the greenhorns look aghast.
The house is not for me;
others will meet on the auction day,
the hammer (touch wood)
hard-headed harbinger of resurrection.

Birds on the Balcony

Five goldfinches today –
such an honour in Camden Town –
perch on the niger feeders,
feast steadily until one is budged
by a flurrying newcomer
in a short, shrill tiff.

Blue tits and great tits
go for the peanuts,
and could that be a wood mouse
shinning up the slippery rod
to have a go at nibbling too?

Intent on your own lives,
what is it that makes you
not just entertaining but so lovable?
We are strangers but kindred
belonging together on Earth.

As I sit in my sunny kitchen
and watch you flitting,
I even think of death
not as lonely disintegration
but remaining part of things,
in atoms and in words.

At the Start

On a sharp blue January noon
chasing days of depressing rain,
along the path past Highgate Ponds
dogs delight in the great puddles,
shuddering their muddy coats in glee.

'No, Rover!', 'No, Plato!'
gasp bespattered owners.
'Black doggy! Messy doggy!'
my grandson calls from his pushchair,
Then: 'Let me out! I want walk!'
Of course he lurches into soggy grass,
crowing: 'Squelch! Squelch! Squelch!'

Back on the tarmac he lumbers
with hunched shoulders: 'Rrrr!
I'm a monster!' emerging from primal slime
into imagination and language,
shambling the long human road.

The buds on the trees are still shut fast
but today seem to promise
something will happen soon,
and from that high branch, voice
like a silver lancet, the robin singing
pierces the soul, the hope,
the pain, the beauty of it.

February Walk

Grey sunless sky and mud.
I heave my heavy body through the park.
Those uncouth cries are flocks of raucous youths
kicking footballs into dusk.
The energies displayed in it are fine.
Their cries in every language sound the same.

Now the light has nearly gone.
My mind shut tight like twigs,
the thin extremities of wintering trees,
it's hard to credit something's pulsing there
or lamb will ever struggle out of dark
to stand and bleat its individual poem.

Longed-for Warmth

How welcome this March sun is
warming my winter body.

The wind has dropped. I lizard
on a wooden bench where lake laps,
water birds glide at ease
and quack a bit, background
noise detracting nothing from a
bonus, peaceful, lazing afternoon.

Only the quick nip
of a less simple neediness.

Colour

For John Milton's 400th Birthday, 2008

Yes, cowslips are back,
a whole carolling bankful
draws me to the lake.
I drink in yellow
pealing from curly bells.
Out of wintriness
my walk quickens
and my spirits blaze.

Vermilion tulips
tremble fleshy and secret
in the stiff breeze
of a chilly April.
I shiver as the living scarlet
pervades my being here,
satisfies desire forgone,
forgotten by starved eyes.

Blue sky and hyacinths,
purple velvet pansies
and every kind of green,
as grass and leaf spring
fresh and sparkle in the sun
when it succeeds in shining
clear of active clouds.
Showers. Rainbow.

Dark, dark, dark,
without all hope of day.
The sun was dark to him,
Milton like his Samson blind,
heart-bleakening lack
of colour, light and joy,
his world cancelled. How come
his poetry never failed?

Bird Sanctuary

Seals sunning themselves,
women all shapes and sizes sprawl
with bird's-foot trefoil, buttercups,
flowering grasses, wild geraniums
and self heal on the lower meadow
of the Ladies' Pond Enclosure.

Whish! goes a kingfisher,
its turquoise matching the dragonfly's,
bird akin to insect as woman is to seal.
On the next pond down, swans,
moorhens, ducks, coots
pursue their wild lives in peace.

It's called the Bird Sanctuary.
Switch off your mobile,
sisters under the skin,
twinned, one pond for ladies
and one is for the birds.

Demonstration

Hyde Park, London, January 10th 2009

The frost bit into bones.
The Old Left grannies were there,
some hobbling in gumboots, shaggy coats,
hand-knitted rainbow scarves
trailed to their knees.

Stamping and blanketed, thousands more
piled past the usual panoply
of paper sellers and thrusting leafleteers
to roar their fury at Gaza dying.
Among the waves of flags and placards
there went the great banner of Jews for Palestine

and among the younger Londoners,
groups of Muslim girls, neatly shod,
nipped waists in fashionable trousers,
pretty scarves tied carefully
and poetic eyes,
danced arm in arm.

'Free Free Palestine!'
they chorused in high thin voices,
like starlings wheeling at sunset,
all the birds of the air a-sighing and a-sobbing,
appalled humanity crying.

Squirrel

'Them squirrels are a blinking nuisance,'
says my neighbour
when they dig up bulbs on her balcony.
I know another
who pops at them with an air gun.

But as I walk through Regent's Park
in the goldening afternoon,
how buoyantly they bounce along,
how delightful their agility at being
up a tree before anyone has twigged.

I crunch through fallen leaves
and see one with its bushy tail
curled against an oak, sitting upright
with an acorn in its paws
and what seems like a beady eye on winter.

Even though it's grey –
dismissed as not the correct kind –
I cannot help loving it,
and feeling glad it's active to survive.
Let it live.

I remember when he saw one
my grandson just learning to talk
sensed an immediate kinship
with his fellow creature
and called out in ecstasy: 'Cyril! Cyril!'

A Londoner

On the bus a laden old lady
sat with her Jack Russell on her lap,
who looked as English as the famous Nipper
listening to His Master's Voice.
'What's your dog's name?' I asked.
'Archie,' which came as no surprise.
Then she added: 'Archimedes.'

I do a double take.
'Eureka!' She flashes me a smile
alight with the intelligence
of ancient Greece. Then I see her
standing with her dog in Syracuse
as that old mathematical philosopher
streaks down the street.

At the School Gates

Towards 3.30 a crowd gathers,
mothers – some have younger ones
in pushchairs or kangarooed in slings
with eyes alert and kicking legs –
grandparents, aunts, childminders,
many more fathers now – one jogs up
from his elsewhere looking rather dazed.

Above the greetings, gossip,
playdate arrangements, local politics,
a large woman gives a music hall belly laugh.
A graceful one in a hijab meets her friend,
still spick and span in office clothes.
Two scruffy grannies in low posh tones
boast of their own with discreet rivalry.

Babble of English accented in a hundred
different voices, the non-native speakers
from many a mother tongue,
this proper London mixture
is here for a single purpose,
all waiting for the iron gates to clang.

Then they surge in to get their children.
In the playground each class has its spot,
the little ones corralled by a picket fence.
Enjoying rhythm, wordplay and fantastic tales,
some are into insects,
others preferring furry animals.

Among the juniors, rangy nine-year-olds
from complex friendships, battles,
sometimes barbaric games,
may be reaching for reason and empathy
with an urge to gather and sort out
the world. They are the future.

The Cleaner

Stefka is tiny with masses of black hair.
Once a week she arrives with a big smile,
calls Etty the cat: 'Etka! Etka!'
and it comes running to her.
Sometimes she brings cat treats
and treats for her ageing employer,
plants, chocolates, Bulgarian biscuits.

After three years she still speaks little English,
is nervous of going to school.
Though not illegal, she has failed
to get a National Insurance number.
Most of the time she works
for a Bulgarian cleaning agency
on a zero hours contract.

At home she was a hairdresser
but here lacks the language for it,
though in her mother tongue her voice
speaks plenty on her mobile phone.
Meanwhile the worn old house
gets the most antagonistic, even affectionate
going over it has ever had.

Toads

Two toads squat in Downing Street.
These are no innocent amphibians,
nor have they hearts of gold, bejewelled heads.
They are not kind princes in disguise;
there will be no turning back,
no metamorphosis.

They hedge their millions craftily,
bank their securities,
while poisoning the body politic
and spitting in the faces of the needy.

As they infect and privatise
the land sickens.
Their slimy ra-ra progress
vandalises many people's lives.
In the media their fleshy faces grin,
they couldn't give a damn.

Cancer as a Political Philosophy

With acknowledgments to Professor Paul Davies, cancer researcher

Cancer behaves as if it had its own
cunning agenda. Rogue cells
run amok around the body,
proliferating uncontrollably.
Tumours use chemical signals to create
cancer-friendly niches in remote organs.

Cancer is not a modern aberration
but has deep evolutionary roots.
For most of Earth's history
life was confined to single-cell organisms.
When at last the multicellular emerged,
the logic of life changed utterly.

In these the body's ordinary cells
outsource their immortality
to specialised germ cells – sperm and egg.
Made by making love,
my child is a new person, is not me;
the price of otherness is death.

Malignant cells break the contract,
have one imperative: to be immortal.
They roll evolution backwards,
as deregulation speeds them
to adopt earlier ancestral forms
of life on Earth a billion year ago.

A throwback to the selfish cell,
they promote themselves above all others,
insist on their own free growth,
mocking the common good
and lethal to the body as a whole.
I don't want to be a single-cell amoeba.

I would rather be a human being.

The Universal Conjugation

Energy, expression and attraction,
we are stardust talking.
We are the same material
as the universe, and its rhythms
from the Big Bang on still beat in us,

as from conception until birth
we re-run the history of life
from single cell to human being,
who not only recapitulates it all
but can become its voice.

Dog roses in the June hedgerow,
each five-petalled bloom blush-pink,
each bush pushes out to its adult shape,
intertwining field maple, hawthorn,
pussy willow, honeysuckle,
to make an ecosystem to inhabit,
creep through, burrow, and for birds
to nest in, chorus on at dawn,
for bees to visit, pollinate.

And what are we among our cousin animals,
the porcupines, the dromedaries, tabby cats?
What is humanity? What can we hope?
Though we muck things up, our ancestry
pushes and enables us
to utter the universe's poem,
the word, the verb, the conjugation:
They are, you are, we are,
we are together, we are one, I AM.

Great Fish

Coming from beds of deep secret roses,
crimson velvet with swoony smell,
I stand by the lake bewitched.
The white, the black and the golden carp
glide silently under the water
at will like thoughts in the early morning
before they are organised
or memories still half submerged
in murky depths. They are so many.
Quick-slipping, their big bodies,
charged with graceful energy,
have the kick of an unborn child,
a person swimming into consciousness
with powerful emotions of the soul.

Epic

From stardust, to simple life, to sex and difference,
then evolution led by love and death,
an altered ape on Earth one day
learned language, longing for so much,
addressed deities, dreamed of paradise.
Consciousness became conscience of shortfall,
there being a battle between brutal thrust
and fellow-feeling, friendly hobnobbing.
Fathomless fears fostered gods,
powers personified disposing of their fate;
offering food to eat was Earth, their mother,
their father the oh-fail-not fiery sun,
and many more imagination shaped,
then over-ruled them all with one supreme.
They held to him to help deliver them
from powerlessness and prayed for prosperous times.

A single supernatural source and mind
enabled them to order all the world
and, making him their model, make a self,
to see themselves as each a single person,
amid flux of feelings and phantasms to say 'I'.
And when their god grew more gracious they began
to imagine humanity might be gracious too,
whole-hearted and healing like him they had created.
But the glimpsed god-led goal eluded them,
the ascent into the unseen was too steep, uncanny.
Deity must come down and dwell on Earth.

His mother was Mary, a man was born
without rank or riches in a rough condition.

Kindness is coming to reign, he proclaimed to the people,
the poor have a privileged place in this kingdom,
heartily shall the hungry feast happy at my table,
the meek, the merciful, the martyrs for justice.
He clashed with clerics who called him a blasphemer,
fought with Pharisees who found him a lawbreaker.
His upside-down gospel upset Empire that killed him.

Then the man Jesus metamorphoses into mythical Christ,
who goes down to the depths of darkness to overcome it,
harrowing hell to hunt out the Devil:

Thou art Doctor of Death, drink that thou madest.
For I that am Lord of Life, love is my drink
and for that drink today I died upon Earth.

Enabling dream, drama and dreadful battle,
now and not yet, needs action and vision.
Doctors of death to be daunted and thwarted,
chancellors challenged who chivvy the poor,
from their lap of luxury, lay burdens on others.

Christ, leading captivity captive, scales the heights,
giver of gifts, true God and true man.
He is seen before he ascends by some of his intimates.
First Mary Magdalene meets him in the garden.
When he breaks bread, this brings recognition.
Be my body by one baked loaf shared,
be of my blood in the bond of this wine,
he cries as he christens re-crowned humankind,
gathering together in goodwill and love
fellow creatures accredited one Christ, one enterprise,
hero of this history of our whole species.

He spreads his spirit spurting tongues of fire,
working its wonders, the word that burns.
Voice of the victims, the invisible who pay,
of the resolute against wrongs, rising again.
All who struggle for strength and strive to do good,
all who love life and lead it generously,
pouring out with passion a poem of being.

Bridegroom and bride are brought to bed,
swooning sweetness of secret bliss.
Primrose and Parliament Hill, St Pancras International,
she shines as a city of social joys,
where communal comfort and kindness reign,
a human habitat, here on this planet.

May Be

Dour, thorny, over-wintered
many ordinary days, once more
this sturdy, modest tree puts out
its curly, first green leaves,
then blossoms white with may,
flesh-scented unforgetting, wedding
hope of pleasant picnic weather,
ponds where we delight to bathe,
Londoners, here on our Heath,

with a sight – in answer
to so many mayday calls –
of a species feasting in kindness,
enjoying its best wine,
humanity together at last
in planetary celebration.

That which is not called amiss
the Good Old Cause
voices the maytree:
belief flowers again.

I climb to the top of Parliament Hill
where kites are flying.
All London spread out below
shines in the beautiful morning.

Habeas Corpus

For Don Cupitt

When I am dead,
were I admitted to heaven
I would not feel at home.
How I would miss the spring.
I sit in an April garden
deep-blue-scented with hyacinths
amid yellow crown imperials.
Would I want a heavy gold crown
for a life achieved? I want this,
which changes every day,
one petal now ragged
where an insect has bitten in,
everything pressing, passing.

How I would miss the summer
with higgledy-piggledy picnics
on the Heath, even when someone
gets lost, arrives late, cross
and it threatens rain.

I prefer that to an angel choir
where I don't belong,
habeas corpus being
sine qua non
of a human song.

Untidy city with your muddle of people
living their lives, not knowing the future.
Earth with your beauty so old and so new,
that does not stay but slays me
again and again with each different recurrence,
kind and careless habitat
where love can flower (or not),
every body lives and dies
and the heart's desire tantalises.
I would be homesick in heaven
and hanker.

The Heart's Sunshine

Arching her back, a girl
practises tightrope walking
between two slender trees.
At last the sun's come out
and Londoners flock to the green Heath.

The ground is a counterpane of picnic parties,
popping corks, young people laughing,
popping strawberries into each other's mouths.
How lovely their supple bodies are, curving
towards each other with unclouded faces.

And the round of generations
toddling, strolling, hobbling,
some swimming in delightful waters,
men and women in their ponds
with dragonflies and water birds.

Love is everywhere on holiday
and this afternoon how beautiful
our languid, energetic species is,
communing and feasting together.
Boys climb oaks and crow triumphantly.

Love moves everything
and the heart leaps to be part of it all,
this expressive humanity,
the poorest now insulted and abused
by feckless powers, the bulling millionaires.

Love sweeps me too.
How can it not? It's the heart's sunshine
that cries out against unkindness
with a vision of happiness, revolution
of the wheel that smoothly turns
to the apt conclusion
of what moves the sun and the other stars.

The Vision Splendid

The sun shines on the whole shape,
each tree, each flower itself,
whether enormous
or a delicate viola,
blissful to contemplate.

How distressed I was
when the sight from my balcony
of that sycamore I called Ygdrasil
was blocked by a narrow house
thrust up between by a developer.

The lust for the whole is overwhelming.
Now I can't see it,
I must console myself
that the tree is still there and I can go
and bow to it in the park,

just as when sight of utopia,
that kind place for all,
is lost, mocked, dismissed
by thrusting dominations,
faith must not fail.

The Buddleia

The buddleia just appeared,
growing out of the wall
of my neighbour's air raid shelter.
It gets bigger and bigger.

Tough, beautiful buddleia,
fountain of purple squirrel tails,
how anarchically there you are,
quietly threatening to infiltrate
that developer's unfitting eyesore
which blocked off my favourite tree.

Blooming lovely buddleia
lit by the evening sun,
how your whole shape satisfies.
Never was weed more welcome.

No Mean City

'All right Dinah?' calls my neighbour
out early walking her dog, as I pass
through St Martin's Gardens to get my paper.
'Morning!' nods Des, rubicund keeper
of the Park. 'Bit nippy,' I reply.
It is November. Sweepers and litter pickers
from Poland, Lithuania, almost anywhere,
are at work with broom, rake and shovel.
More exchanges. 'Brrr! it's cold!' 'And damp!'
Later tidy office workers will hurry along,
and mothers hustling children to school.
A tall African father brings his family
early enough for a go on the swings.

Squarely at his door stands Nusrat,
the shopkeeper, having his morning smoke
with black coffee (the best in Camden)
from the next-door caff, whence news
pours out in Portuguese
to pavement tables, people breakfasting.
As I enter his shop, he sacrifices his cig
burning away on the ashtray outside
and comes in to serve me. 'You OK, mammy?'
he greets me, as on his telly they argue in Turkish.
Then to the Little Baker's I go to get croissants
and a small loaf. In her red-striped apron
Hand, the Egyptian assistant, looks anxious.
I tell her the campers in St Paul's churchyard
have put up a sign saying Tahir Square.
She grins. London is waking up.

The nights are colder now.
Red, blue and green,
some neat, some scruffy,
at the great west door of the cathedral,
round-bellied, pregnant tents
are growing the word,
repeat Mary's Magnificat:

> *put down the mighty from their seats,*
> *lift up the lowly,*
> *the hungry filled with good things,*
> *the rich sent empty away.*

Rainsborough at the Putney Debates of 1647:

> *The poorest he that is in England*
> *hath a life to live, as the greatest he.*

Giles Fraser, Vicar of St Mary's Putney
where the debates took place,
afterwards Canon Chancellor of St Paul's,
resigned because he couldn't stomach
those pregnant tents ripped open
and smashed down.
In the churchyard of St Paul the tentmaker

> *the word was made flesh and pitched its tent among us.*

Published 'at the Sign of the black Spread Eagle
at the west end of Pauls, 1649',
Winstanley's *Watchword to the City of London and the Army:*

> *The Earth should be made a common treasury*
> *of livelihood to whole mankind,*
> *without respect of persons.*

Blake's two poems called 'Holy Thursday'.
First, sweetly:

'Twas on a Holy Thursday, their innocent faces clean,
The children walking two and two, in red and blue and green.
Grey headed beadles walked before, with wands as white as snow
Till into the high dome of Paul's they like Thames waters flow.

Second, furiously:

Is this a holy thing to see
In a rich and fruitful land,
Babes reduced to misery,
Fed with cold and usurous hand?

Is that trembling cry a song?
Can it be a song of joy?
And so many children poor?
It is a land of poverty!

And still so many children poor.
In rich and fruitful England
child poverty increasing, inflation,
Sure Start schemes fold quietly,

London Bridge is falling down.

The sound of infant singing dies,
libraries, community centres closing,
the National Health stealthily privatised,
an ailing, ragged body politic,
a social fabric unravelling.
It is a land of poverty.

Bankers' pay goes on getting bigger,
bonuses claimed as of right –
a cabinet of millionaires
won't tax those parasites,
the ever-widening great gulf.

Help us to save free conscience from the paw
Of hireling wolves, whose gospel is their maw,

roars John Milton, Londoner, born near St Paul's.
And from Lambeth William Blake re-echoes him:

Is this thy soft family love
Thy cruel patriarchal pride,
Planting thy family alone,
Destroying all the World beside?

Falling towers
Athens Rome Madrid Lisbon London
thrones dominations principalities powers
visible and invisible *archai, exousiai,*
real and unreal City Market Money
post o'er land and ocean without rest,
swiftly, silently dispose of all our lives and deaths.

The idols of the heathen are silver and gold.
They do not cry in their throats.

Human beings cry.
Everywhere voices sobbing,
often unheard. 'I've lost my job,
they've laid off two hundred.'
'We're being repossessed,
we'll lose our home.'

'I've tried and tried to find work
but still no luck.'
'I signed on two months ago
and nothing has come through.
Panic. Can we live on air?'
'We can't stay in this flat,
housing benefit won't pay for it.
Must we live in Luton
where we know no one at all?'
'On this money take your choice:
heat or eat. Dread the winter.'
'The kids keep whining.
The price of shoes!'
'An old woman froze to death.'
'A young father hanged himself
in St Martin's Gardens.
We saw him dangling.
Later we heard bare details of his story,
nothing more.'

Someone shat in St Paul's.
'We are the scum of the Earth,
the off-scouring,' said St Paul,
human filth, for a moment,
made visible in his cathedral.
Down-and-out, often unseen,
half-crazed wanderers
haunt the chartered streets.
London cries weep weep weep.
Jesus said:

> *Blessed are you who are poor,*
> *for yours is the kingdom.*

Unless it is good news for the poor,
the *anawim,* it is not the kingdom,
it is not the beautiful city.

> *And I saw the holy city, New Jerusalem,*
> *coming down from heaven,*
> *dressed as a bride for her husband.*
> *The dwelling of God is with humans.*

The crying will cease,
the tears will be wiped away.
The marriage of Christ the Lamb
to the shining city, made one
divine humanity.

> *The fields from Islington to Marybone,*
> *To Primrose Hill and St John's Wood,*
> *Were builded over with pillars of gold*
> *And there Jerusalem's pillars stood.*

> *Her little ones ran on the fields,*
> *The Lamb of God among them seen,*
> *And fair Jerusalem his Bride*
> *Among the little meadows green.*

In his *Oracle upon Managua,*
his own city earthquake-struck,
Ernesto Cardenal says:

> *After all God is also city...*
> *the free city*
> *where God is everybody*
> *He, God-with-everybody (Emmanuel)*
> *the universal City*
> *the City where God's humanity is revealed to us...*

And Yahweh said: I am not.
I will be. I am the one who will be, he said.
I am Yahweh a God who waits in the future
(who cannot be unless the conditions are right)
God who is not but who WILL BE
for he is love-among-humans
and he is not, he WILL BE.

Come and do not delay.
In the reverse acrostic of the Great O Antiphons:
ERO CRAS, I will be tomorrow.

Already in ordinary lives
all the loving that goes on,
not always, but plenty,
all the creativity.
The baby gazes into his mother's face
as she smiles at him and says his name.
She is his looking glass.
On Hampstead Heath
a young lad and his father climb a tree.
'Grab that branch!' Protective
but not nervy or over-cautious.
Couples, not all young, hold hands,
nest on the Heath in summer:
'Darling, this is the best day of my life.'
An aunt says of her two nephews:
'They're funny boys and I love them to bits.'
She pours herself out,
chatting and joking with them
when she gets them from school.
A Sure Start worker chanting
nursery rhymes in the warm library,
helped a child with poor English
at least to clap the rhythm,
smiled at the scarved, shy mum:

Build it up with sticks and stones!

The tea dance in Finsbury Town Hall:
'Would you care to have a whirl?'
Love for the difficult, the addict,
the batty old woman (I look at her
and see myself before too long).
She comes to the door:
'I've lost my teeth. Who are you?'
Love unreciprocated,
the agony of being dumped:
'He doesn't want me any more.'
All the endurance and complications,
the pain and delight of loving, which daily
go on and on and on.

Not fragments shored against my ruins
but love, builder of cities,
city of communion,
sturdy and graceful public structure
a necessity for lives to abound,
not be thwarted, distorted, wasted.

City of voices
thronging the air over centuries,
Rainsborough, Winstanley, Milton, Blake,
144 thousand, that's far from all,
voices protesting against injustice,
voices pleading, needing to be heard,
everyday voices speaking now,
city of 300 languages and more,
from Poland, Lithuania, Portugal,
Turkey, Egypt, Libya, Ethiopia,
Somalia, India, Japan, Iraq,
Brazil, Peru, almost anywhere.

In my exchanges every land
Shall walk, and mine in every land
Mutual shall build Jerusalem
Both heart in heart and hand in hand.

Inexhaustible utopian vision.
Epic of Christ the Universal Humanity,
myth and metaphor of incarnation.
Word embodied, God become human
raised above the thrones and dominations,
principalities and powers,
above the idols of silver and gold.
(A placard in St Paul's churchyard:
REGULATE BANKS.)
Gold is for building the city,
for the work of building the city.

Build it up with silver and gold!

Christ with Jerusalem his bride,
the garden city of human kindness.

The city is pure gold, clear as glass...
the river of the water of life, bright as crystal,
flows through the middle of the street of the city.
On either side of the river is the tree of life
with its twelve kinds of fruit...
and the leaves of the tree are for the healing of nations.

City where humankind can grow to its potential
male and female human form divine,
because each human being can flower.

And suddenly a sound from heaven
like a rushing mighty wind,
tongues of fire resting on each of them.
Speaking and being understood by

> *Parthians and Medes and Elamites*
> *and residents of Mesopotamia,*
> *Judea and Cappadocia,*
> *Pontus and Asia,*
> *Phyrgia and Pamphylia,*
> *Egypt and visitors from Rome,*
> *Cretans and Arabians.*

God is love who cannot be
except as love-among-humans.
Now and not yet, emergent
God with us, Emmanuel,
when the spirit of kindness reigns
over the beloved city.

Common

'Common as dirt those horrid people are,'
she cried. She was the snobbiest of snobs,
opined in high thin voice that carried far:
'The working classes are such hopeless slobs.
They always drink weak coffee and strong tea,
while we would never do a thing like that.'
For some years now she's shared the common fate,
reduced to dirt, since all that lives must die.
I think how life arose from cosmic dust,
how even in poor soil nasturtiums thrive –
their salad leaves. I drink pure orange gold
in sunlit blissfulness, which in one burst
extols the commonwealth of things alive,
the multimillions this strong bond can hold.

*

With shadows playing on its trunk
green willow changes me.
Through water rippling dapple brown
I swim eternity.

Hampstead Heath is common land
where conversations sprout
from fauna strangely stirring love,
enjoying their time out.

The unripe grapes on garden wall
are bitter till they fill.
The fuchsia dangles for the bee.
Home now I sit still.

*

Assault is not uncommon near this tube
when darkness covers common criminals
and desperate junkies mug a mug to grab
a purse for drugs, mainline or little pills.
Awoken, wonder what is going on –
at two o'clock there's shouting in the street:
A late night revel? Sounds more like a fight –
I toss and mutter, then the noise has gone.
And now I wake to music, singing birds;
cheerfulness and light are breaking in.
Then just before I get my breakfast tray
I cross the park and hear familiar words:
'All right?' 'Good morning.' Ghosts retreat again
as people greet the growth of common day.

*

This ordinary morning springs
a pink and scented rose,
enfolding soul's utmost desire
near common labourers.

Who start at eight, skilled trades come too,
all muscling to repair
our dusty London terraces
with banging and with care.

A toddler runs on sturdy legs
and covers quite some ground.
His watching mother smiles but feels
lonely for a friend.

*

The supper was delicious in the dusk,
hungry from work, first drink was heavenly,
the outlined twilit trees, the earthy musk
and even better was the company.
When there is much in common, deep exchange
of thoughts and musing quickens with delight;
as garden robin listens, insects flit,
the sudden insights dart and inklings range.
And in another garden sat a pair.
He, such a good cook, had taken pains,
she was attracted but was playing cool.
Old comrades now becoming something more?
Take it easy, girl, what if it rains?
Or will he kiss her with the strawberry fool?

*

All can become one body if
one common loaf is shared.
He said, 'This is my body. Eat,'
and offered common bread.

Two can be joined together when
they share a common bed.
Christ the human form divine
the bridegroom and his bride.

She is the city, beautiful
and hearing every need,
where every tear is wiped away,
all want the common good.

*

Dreamscaped by long imagination
this metaphor, utopia, state of grace
urges change required, the transformation
of unjust structures, all that they deface.
Quite unrefined, a criminal, and he
enjoyed his grub, he had the common touch,
the mythic metamorphosis of such
material of common humanity.
Perhaps that can never be achieved:
we are so mixed. But feelings of it shine
in common or garden London every day,
accomplished work, love given and received,
both build cities: what is yours is mine
in times of happiness, pure poetry.

*

God the idea of the good
becoming commonplace,
residing in the human breast,
the city and the house.

Nothing supernatural then
for it has been dispersed
in nature – with its humankind
together the whole Christ.

Eternity in common time,
not always, here and there.
Common measure this refrain
and this is common prayer.

NOTES

At the Start (p.23):
'And a sword will pierce your own soul too.'
– Luke 2:35. Simeon's words in the Temple to Mary, the mother of Jesus.

February Walk (p.24):
'Though a quarrel in the streets is a thing to be hated, the energies displayed in it are fine; the commonest man shows grace in his quarrel.'
– John Keats, Letter to George and Georgiana Keats, 19th March 1819.

Colour (p.27):
'O dark, dark, dark, amid the blaze of noon,
Irrecoverably dark, total eclipse
Without all hope of day!...
The sun to me is dark...'
– Milton, *Samson Agonistes,* 80–86.
The poem was written for John Milton's 400th birthday festival in Chalfont St Giles in 2008.

Cancer as a Political Philosophy (p.36):
Paul Davies, article in *The Guardian,* 18th November 2012. Paul Davies is the director of the Beyond Center for Fundamental Concepts in Science at Arizona State University.

Epic (p.40):
Lines in italic *'Thou art Doctor of Death ...'* are from *Piers Plowman,* passus XVIII, 365-7.

May Be (p.43):

'What I have spoken, is the language of that which is not called amiss the Good Old Cause.'
– John Milton, *The Ready and Easy Way to Establish a Free Commonwealth,* published in February 1660, shortly before the Restoration.

Habeas Corpus (p.44):

In Peter Abelard's hymn about heaven, *O Quanta Qualia,* he says:
'Nec ineffabiles cessabunt jubili
quos decantabimus et nos et angeli.
There'll be no end of unutterable praises
we and the angels together shall sing.'
Without bodies the praises will be unutterable.

The Heart's Sunshine (p.47):

'Ma già volgeva il mio disio e'l velle
si come rota ch'igualmente è mossa
l'amor che move il sole e l'altre stelle.'
'But now what ran my will and my desires,
like a smoothly turning wheel, was
love that moves the sun and the other stars.'
– Dante, *Paradiso,* canto 33.

No Mean City (p.57):

ERO CRAS. The 7 Great O antiphons, each containing the words 'O ... come' with a different title of Christ, are sung at vespers/evensong on the successive days leading up to Christmas. Listed backwards from Christmas, the Christ titles are: O **E**mmanuel (God with Us), O **R**ex Gentium (King of the Nations), O **O**riens (Dayspring), O **C**lavis David (Key of David), O **R**adix Jesse (Root of Jesse), O **A**donai (Lord), O **S**apientia (Wisdom).The Latin initials form the words *ero cras:* I will be tomorrow.